MW00780560

QUIET MOMENTS WITH HILDEGARD AND THE WOMEN MYSTICS

QUIET MOMENTS WITH HILDEGARD
AND THE WOMEN MYSTICS

120 DAILY READINGS

CHARIS

SERVANT PUBLICATIONS
ANN ARBOR, MICHIGAN

© 1999 by Servant Publications

Charis Books is an imprint of Servant Publications especially designed to serve Roman Catholics.

Published by Servant Publications
P.O. Box 8617
Ann Arbor, Michigan 48107

Cover design: Left Coast Design, Portland, Oregon
Cover illustration: Hildegard of Bingen detail from *The Four Seasons.* Used by permission of Art Resource.

99 00 01 02   10 9 8 7 6 5 4 3 2 1

Printed in the United States of America
ISBN 0-56955-140-5

LIBRARY OF CONGRESS CATALOGING-IN-PUBLICATION DATA

Quiet moments with Hildegard and the women mystics / compiled by Evelyn Bence.
    p.   cm.
  Includes bibliographical references.
  ISBN 1-56955-140-5 (alk. paper)
  1. Mysticism—Catholic Church.   2. Women mystics.   3. Spiritual life—Catholic Church.   I. Bence, Evelyn, 1952–
BV5082.2.Q54   1999
248.2′2—dc21   99-26263
                                                         CIP

CONTENTS

INTRODUCTION

Mystical grace. The women presented in these pages had one basic commonality: They were in love with the Trinitarian God, whom they knew in extraordinarily intimate ways. God talked to them. God walked with them. God told them they were His own.

Not that this was an easy road. Many reveled in spiritually passionate ecstasies but alternately suffered intense physical pain and emotional anguish. They were well aware of spiritual enemies and saw themselves as sinners plucked from the fire—by grace, for love, and for a purpose. Their love for God compelled them to love the sorrowful creatures in their world who, like them, were made of dirt and dust.

Fortunately, these women were able to write what they'd seen, dictate what they'd heard, and teach what they'd learned, so we can learn of and from them. Some living in convents carried on extensive correspondence. In or out of the cloister, some had well-placed enemies who tried to squelch their writing or work. A few fought for and effected reform of abuses in the clergy and Church.

I've chosen to organize this collection of writings of women mystics more or less chronologically, from the twelfth century through a historical succession into the eighteenth century. Is this lineup exhaustive? Not at all. In more recent times has God turned silent? By no means. But books have deadlines and a predetermined number of pages, and so I offer this sampling as just that—a sampling of quiet, reflective moments with Hildegard and other women mystics.

Evelyn Bence

Saint Hildegard
of Bingen
1098-1179

Hildegard, the tenth and youngest child of a noble German family, entered a Benedictine convent at age eight. Eventually a formidable abbess, she was a composer, painter, naturalist and physician, preacher, prophet, politician, and extraordinary visionary. These selections are from her Scivias (Know the Ways), describing twenty-six visions. "I saw with the interior eyes of my spirit, and I heard with my interior ears, and not in dreams nor in ecstasy."

1. Explaining the Trinity

As the flame in one fire has three powers, so the one God is in three Persons. In what manner? For in the flame abides splendid light, innate vigor, and fiery heat. It has splendid light that it may shine, innate vigor that it may flourish, and fiery heat that it may burn. So consider in the splendid light, the Father who in His paternal love sheds His light upon the faithful. In that innate vigor of the splendid flame in which that same flame shows its power, understand the Son, who took flesh from the Virgin, in which the Divinity declared His wonders. And in the fiery heat, behold the Holy Spirit, who gently kindles the hearts and minds of the faithful....

Therefore as in one flame these three powers are discerned, so in the unity of the Divinity three Persons are to be understood.

2. Our Intentions Known to God

People have in themselves struggles between confession and denial. In what way? Because some confess Me and some deny Me. And in the struggle the question is: Is there a God or not? Then the question is answered inwardly by the Holy Spirit: "There is a God who created you and redeemed you." And as long as this answer to the question is in a person, the power of God is not wanting in that person, because that person adheres in penitence to this question and answer.

But when this question is not in a person, neither is the answer of the Holy Spirit, because that person has expelled the gift of God; without this question asked in penitence, this person precipitates himself into death. But the Virtues [an order of angels] offer the contests of these battles to God, because they are like a seal in the presence of God, in which is shown to God whether He is worshiped or denied in intention.

3. Consider Good and Evil

The choirs of angels sing, "You are just, O Lord!" [Ps 119:137], because God's justice has no flaw in it; for God delivered Man not by power but by mercy, when He sent His Son into the world to redeem him. No smear of dung soils the sun; and likewise no wickedness of injustice can touch God. But you, O human, with reflective knowledge consider good and evil. What are you when you soil yourself with many desires of the flesh? And what are you when the brightest gems of the virtues shine in you?…

But you, O human, when you consider good and evil, are standing, as it were, where two roads branch off. If you despise the darkness of evil and want to see Him whose creature you are, and whom you acknowledged in holy baptism where the old sin of Adam was nullified in you; and if you say, "I want to fly from the Devil and his works and follow the true God and His precepts"; then think how you have been taught to turn away from evil and do good, and how the Heavenly Father did not spare His Only-Begotten but sent Him for your deliverance; and pray to God to help you.

4. The Soul and the Flesh

The soul is the mistress, the flesh the handmaid. How? The soul rules the body by vivifying it, and the body is ruled by this vivification, for if the soul did not vivify the body it would fall apart and decay. But when a person does an evil deed and the soul knows it, it is as bitter for the soul as poison is for the body when it knowingly takes it. But the soul rejoices in a sweet deed as the body delights in sweet food. And the soul flows through the body like sap through a tree. What does this mean? By the sap, the tree grows green and produces flowers and then fruit. And how is this fruit matured? By the air's tempering. How? The sun warms it, the rain waters it, and thus by the tempering of the air it is perfected. What does this mean? The mercy of God's grace, like the sun, will illumine the person; the breath of the Holy Spirit, like the rain, will water him; and so discernment, like the tempering of the air, will lead him to the perfection of good fruits.

5. Reading the Stars?

No human being has a star of his own, which determines his life, as a foolish and erring people tries to assert; all stars are at the service of all people. That star [of Bethlehem] only shone more brightly than all other stars because My Only-Begotten, unlike all other humans, was born without sin from a virgin birth. But that star gave My Son no aid, except in faithfully announcing His Incarnation to the people; for all stars and other creatures, fearing Me, fulfil My command, but do not have any knowledge of anything about any creature. For creatures fulfill My commands when it pleases Me, in the same way as when a minter, making a coin, strikes it with the requisite form; then that coin displays the form stamped on it, but has no power to know when the minter may decide to impress another form on it....

Neither stars nor fire nor birds nor any other creatures of this kind can either harm you or help you by your examining them.

6. Marital Fidelity

God in His secret wisdom graciously formed this union of male and female for the propagation of people. And because He so rightly constituted this union, foolish human desire should not cause a breach between the two parts, and neither part should take the dowry of its blood to an alien place; for, as God commanded that people should not slay each other, He also commanded that they should not divert their blood from its rightful place by cruel fornication.

Therefore, let people repress the ardor of their longing and not transmit their flame to an alien fire. For if an ardent will takes hold of the will of another and stirs it up to fervent lust for a stronger or weaker reason, the two will coalesce into one by the first person's mental desire and the other's consent to be embraced by it. For the sight of the outer eye makes the inner heat burst into flame. And even if the one body does not sin with the other, the living will still makes them burn, so that all their viscera are shaken by their feelings. Therefore, let the outer person be guarded with such caution that the inner person may never be wounded by carelessness.

7. I Am Present

I the Father am present to every creature and withdraw Myself from none; but you, O human, do withdraw yourself from creatures. For instance, when you look into water, your face appears in it, but your reflection can exercise none of your powers, and when you turn away you no longer appear in the water. But I do not appear to creatures thus changeably; I am present to them in a true manifestation, never withdrawing My power from them but doing in them by the strength of My will whatever I please. And so too I truly display My majesty in the sacrament of the body and blood of My Son, and wondrously perform My miracles there from the beginning of the priest's secret words until the time when that mystery is received by the people.

8. Matters of Life and Death

I, O human, knew you before the foundation of the world. Nevertheless, I will consider your days in your works and judge of their usefulness, and diligently and sharply examine your deeds. But if I suddenly withdraw anyone from this life, the usefulness of his life is complete; and if his life were extended longer, it would not keep on in freshness bearing good fruits but, tainted by the faith of the flesh, would only give off smoke like the empty sound of words and not attain to Me in the inmost depth of its heart. Therefore I do not grant him a prolongation of this life, but withdraw him from this world before he falls into the apathy of this infertility. But to you, O human, I say: Why do you despise Me? Did I not send My prophets to you, and give My Son on the wood of the cross for your salvation, and choose My apostles to show you the way of truth through the gospel? So, having all good things through Me, you cannot excuse yourself. And why then do you put Me off?

9. The Last Day

The divine commandment to rise again being obeyed, as was shown to you, the bones of the dead, wherever they were, in the flash of an eye joined together, each in its place, are covered with their flesh, nor are they hindered in any way; whether they were consumed by fire, by water, by birds, or by beasts, they are restored most quickly, because the earth gave them up in that manner in which salt drips from water....

So all humans in the twinkling of an eye shall rise again in body and in soul, without any contradiction or cutting off of their members, but in the integrity both of their bodies and of their sex, the elect having the glory of their good works, and the wicked bearing the blackness of their unhappy deeds, so that their works are not hidden there, but will appear openly in themselves.

And certain of these were signed in faith....

But certain had not the sign of faith, because they did not wish to have any knowledge of the living and true God, either under the old law or the new grace.

10. Song to Mary

O most splendid gem! The serene beauty of the sun is poured into you, the fountain springing from the heart of the Father, which is the only begotten Word, through whom He created the primary material of the world, which Eve troubled: He made this Word Man in you, and you are that brilliant gem, from whom that Word brought forth all the virtues and in that primary matter produced all creatures.

O sweetest rod, bringing forth leaves from the root of Jesse. Oh, how great is the virtue the Divinity saw in this most beautiful daughter, as an eagle fixes his eye upon the sun, when the Father above regarded the excellency of the Virgin, when He willed that His Word should be incarnate in her. For the soul of the Virgin being illuminated in a hidden mystery of God, the bright Flower issued from this same Virgin in a wonderful way.

Saint Clare of Assisi
1194-1253

At age eighteen Clare ran away from her comfortable home to join up with Francis of Assisi, preaching the way of poverty and abandonment. She and other female followers moved into a church rebuilt by Francis. At his urging they founded the Order of the Poor Ladies (Poor Clares). She was the first known woman to write a "rule" for a religious community.

11. Love, Pray, and Persevere

Love with your whole hearts the good God, who deserves our love above all things, and love His dear Son, who for us poor sinners was nailed to the cross. Let nothing hinder you from constantly thinking of God in your hearts. Meditate continually on the mysteries of His sufferings and upon the sorrows of His blessed mother, standing at the foot of the cross. Watch and pray without ceasing. Be ever careful to persevere in the good course you have begun. Fulfill the ministry, with which you have been charged, in entire poverty and sincere humility. Fear not, my dearest daughter! "The Lord is faithful in all his words, and holy in all his works" (Ps 145:14). He will pour out upon you and your daughters the abundance of His divine blessing. He will be your Helper and Consoler, your Savior, and your everlasting exceedingly great Reward.

12. Sisterly Advice

I pray you to remain faithful until death to Him to whom you have consecrated your lives, and be assured that, in recompense of your labors, you will obtain the crown of everlasting life. Remember that the time of trial and of sufferings is short and that, on the other hand, the happiness in store for you will last forever. Let not the tumult and pomp of the world have aught to do with you; for the world passes away like a shadow. Be not carried away with its flattering appearances, for they are deceitful. The old serpent will hiss and try to frighten you. "But resist the devil and he will flee from you" (Jas 4:7). Be not discouraged by adversity, neither puffed up with success; by its nature faith keeps a soul humble in success and makes it strong in adversity. Faithfully render to God what you have promised Him by your vows, and be exact in doing so, for He knows how to recompense your sacrifice. Look up to heaven, which invites you to take up the cross and follow Christ, who walks before you.

13. Letter to the Princess of Bohemia

It is true then that you have trampled underfoot the most brilliant honors, the most enviable glory of the world, even the throne of the august emperor to whom you might have become allied, and that you have embraced with your whole soul and with intense desire holy poverty, the subduing of the flesh, and the lowly estate of our divine Redeemer, whom you have chosen for your inheritance. Have confidence! God will enable you, by His grace, to preserve intact the priceless treasure of virginity. His power is above all other power. His amiability transcends that of any other being. His beauty casts into shade whatever is most beautiful. His love satisfies all desires, and is worth more than all earthly delight.

How happy you are, therefore, to have been chosen by this divine Bridegroom who, in the style of the language of sacred Scripture, has adorned your neck with precious stones, your ears with rings of inestimable value, your breast with a cincture of purest gold, your brow with a dazzling crown, marked with the seal of holiness.

14. O Blessed Poverty

O blessed Poverty, to which is promised the kingdom of heaven and glory everlasting!

O blessed Poverty, which gives to those who love and embrace you such priceless goods and a life so happy and so free of all unrest!

O amiable Poverty, which has been loved so especially and so tenderly, and has been embraced so fondly by our Lord who has created all things by one word of His mouth, who has governed them, and will govern them all days with sovereign power! He Himself said, "The foxes have holes and the birds of the air nests, but the Son of Man has nowhere to lay his head" (Mt 8:20). And in truth, from the day on which the divine Lord descended into the womb of a pure virgin to unite Himself to our humanity, He was made poor and needy, so that people who were poor and needy in heavenly goods might be made rich with the treasures of His grace and possess the kingdom of heaven.

15. Spiritual Combat

You know that when we love the things of this earth we lose the fruit of divine love, and that we cannot serve two masters at one and the same time, without displeasing either the one or the other. You know that he who is impeded by his garments cannot compete in combat with one who is naked; we cannot hope to fight successfully without stripping ourselves entirely; earthly adornments are only means in the hands of our enemy to lay hold on us more easily. Yes, my sister, it is difficult to live in luxury in this world and to reign with Christ in the other. "It is easier for a camel to pass through the eye of a needle than for a rich man to enter into the kingdom of heaven" (Mt 19:24). You have, therefore, done well to cast aside these superfluous garments, that is, the good of this earth. You will now be able to overcome all the more easily the enemy's attacks.

Blessed Angela of Foligno
1248-1309

An Italian widow and Third-Order Franciscan, Angela with one companion was cloistered in a house, where many disciples came to pray and consult with her. Frequent ecstasies and visions that took her to the depths of Christ's suffering heightened her natural senses and intensified her love for God.

16. Liberty Within the Rule

Be on your guard against those who say they have the spirit of liberty, but who are not following the way of Christ, who was made under the law, although He was the giver of the law. He who was free was made a slave, and therefore it is necessary for those who would follow Christ to conform themselves to the life of Christ, not in seeking liberty by loosening the law and the precepts of God, as many do, but by subjecting themselves to the law and precepts of God, and even to His counsels. And let them make for themselves a circle, and this circle will give them a rule, that is, the Holy Spirit will give them a rule how they ought to live, and it will bind them, for many things might be lawful for them to do, which are not contrary to God, but which the Holy Spirit suffers them not to do.

17. I Am Meek and Humble of Heart

"Learn," [Jesus] said, "of me" (Mt 11:29). But He did not say, "for I fast," although He for our example fasted forty days and forty nights. Nor did He say, "Learn to despise the world, and to live in poverty," although He lived in the greatest poverty and commanded His disciples to live in the same. Nor did He say, "Learn of me, how I made the heavens." Nor did He say, "Learn of me how to work miracles," or any such things, although He by His own power worked miracles and would have His disciples also work miracles in His name. But He simply said this: "for I am meek and humble of heart," as if he would say, "If I have not shown you an example of humility by deed and word, believe me not." And again, in a wonderful way did He set before us an example in this matter, and provoke us to look to the example of His humility and to shape all our actions upon it.

18. One Step to Peace With God

I came into the church and asked God to grant me some grace. While I was praying and saying the Our Father, God Himself put the Our Father into my heart with so great a clearness and understanding of the goodness of God and my own unworthiness, as would be out of my power to express. Moreover, each word was explained to me in my heart, and I spoke it with great slowness and contrition and compunction, so that although on the one hand I wept on account of my sins and my unworthiness, which I knew to be there, yet had I great consolation, and I began to taste somewhat of the sweetness of God, because in the Our Father, I understood better than in any other thing the goodness of God, and I still find it there better than in anything else. Also in the Our Father, my sins and unworthiness were shown to me, and I began to be so ashamed as not to dare to lift up my eyes to heaven, or to the crucifix, or to any other thing.

19. God Is Love

God said that … He requires nothing but that the soul seek
Him and love Him, because He Himself truly loves the soul,
and He is Himself her love.

That God is the love of the soul He showed me in a lively
manner, by His advent, and by the cross, which He bore for
us…. And He unfolded to me His passion, and the other things
He did for us. And He added: "See, then, if in Me there be anything else but love." Then my soul understood for certain that
He was nothing but love. He complained, however, that at
that time, He found so few people in whom to place His grace,
and He said that now He would give far greater grace to those
whom He found loving Him, than up to this time He had
given to the other saints who have lived. Then again He said
to me: "My sweet daughter, love Me, because you are much
more loved by Me than I by thee. O My loved one, love Me!"

20. God's Power and Presence

"I will show you of My power."

And the eyes of my soul were opened, and I saw a certain plenitude of God, in which I comprehended all the world, that which is beyond the sea and on this side of the sea and the sea itself and the abyss and all things, in which I saw nothing but the power of God in a manner utterly unutterable. And my soul, in its exceeding wonder, cried out and said: "Behold, the world is pregnant with God!" And I comprehended all the world as if it were some little thing. And I saw that the power of God exceeds and fills all things. And He said, "You have seen somewhat of My power, now see My lowliness." And I saw so deep a stooping down of God toward mankind, and so great a lowliness, that my soul accounted itself as wholly nothing.... And I began to account myself unworthy of Communion.... He said: "Behold, now the Power is on the altar, and I am within you, and if you receive Me, you receive Me whom you have already received. Communicate, therefore, in the name of the Father, and of the Son, and of the Holy Spirit, and I, who am worthy, make you worthy."

21. Consolation at Eucharist

A voice from God spoke to me and said, "Behold, all good is in you, and you go to receive all good." I began to think: *If all good is in me, why do I go to receive?* And straightaway I received the answer: "One thing does not exclude the other." And when I drew nigh to communicate, it was said to me: "Now is the Son of God upon the altar, both according to His humanity and according to His Godhead, and He is accompanied by a multitude of angels." And when I had a great desire of seeing Him with the angels, as had been said to me, then was God shown to me, as I saw Him. But I saw Him not in the likeness of any form, but I saw a fullness, a beauty, and in the midst thereof, I saw all good. And it was said to me: "O Beloved, so shall you stand before Him in life everlasting." The greatness of the consolation my soul received cannot be explained.

22. Give Me a Sign
to Draw Me out of Doubt

I asked that God would give me or speak some corporal sign ... that He should put in my hand a candle or a precious stone ... or that He should give me any other sign, as He willed, promising that I would not show this sign except as He indicated.

He answered, "What you ask for is a sign that would give you joy only when you touch it, but it would not draw you out of doubt, and in such a sign you might be deceived. But I will give you a sign better than you ask for; this sign shall be continually with you, inwardly in your soul, and you shall always feel it. This shall be the sign: You shall ever be fervent in love and in the love of God and enlightened by the knowledge of God within you. Let this be a most certain sign for you, because none can make this sign except Me. This is the sign I place inwardly in your soul: I place in you a love of Me, by which your soul will become inebriated and fervent and constantly glowing by reason of Me, so that you will desire to suffer tribulations for the love of Me."

23. Mary and the Infant Jesus at the Temple

I saw Our Lady entering the Temple, and my soul went to meet her with great reverence and love. When I was afraid to come near her, Our Lady gave my soul great security and held out to me her Son, Jesus. She said, "O lover of my Son, take Him!" She delivered her Son into my arms. He seemed to have His eyes closed, as if He slept, and He was wrapped in swaddling clothes.

Our Lady sat down as if wearied by her journey. She made such beautiful and pleasing signs ... that my soul not only regarded the Child Jesus ... but was forced also to look upon Our Lady. While I stood there, suddenly the Child seemed naked in my arms and opened and shut His eyes. In the look of those eyes I felt and had such love that it wholly overcame me. For from those eyes went forth an unspeakably great splendor and fire of love and joy. Then there appeared an immense ineffable majesty, and He said to me: "He who has not seen Me little, has not seen Me great." He added, "I have come to you and offered Myself to you, that you may offer yourself to Me."

24. One Holy Thursday...

I said to my companion that we should go and look for Christ. And she said, "Let us go to the hospital, and perchance we shall find Christ among the poor, and the suffering, and the afflicted." We took off all our head cloths, as far as we could (for we had nothing else), and told the waiting woman of the hospital to sell them, and to buy something for the poor of the hospital to eat. Although she refused for a long time to do this and said that we were bringing disgrace upon ourselves, yet, because we pressed her, she went and sold those poor little cloths, and with the money she bought some fish. We ourselves brought bread that had been given us by the love of God for our food. After we had offered these things to the poor, we washed the feet of the poor women living there, and the hands of the men, especially of a certain leper, whose hands were very fetid, withered, and cramped. We then drank of the water with which we had washed him. In that draught we felt such sweetness that we went all the way back in great sweetness, and I tasted a wonderful sweetness.

25. Three Kinds of Prayer

The prayer of the body is continually joined with the sound of words and exercise of the body, as for instance genuflections and bowings. And this kind of prayer I never lay aside, for at times when I have desired to exercise mental prayer, I have been deceived and impeded by sloth and sleep; therefore I exercise myself in the prayer of the body. But this kind of prayer leads into mental prayer, which ought to be made with attention; when you say the Our Father, consider what you say, without running over the words and striving to complete a certain number, like poor little women who do so much work for a given price.

Mental prayer is that in which God so occupies the mind that it thinks of nothing else.... This prayer cuts off the tongue, so that it cannot speak, for the mind is so full of God that it cannot occupy itself in thinking of anything but God. So from this mental prayer the soul arrives at that which is supernatural.

Supernatural prayer is that in which the soul is so lifted up by this thought and fullness of God, that she is stretched above her own nature and comprehends more of God than by her own nature she is able to comprehend.

Saint Gertrude
the Great
1256-1301

From early childhood Gertrude lived at the Benedictine abbey at Helfta, Germany. Her writings describe a spiritual conversion at age twenty-five. Like many mystics, she felt "chosen" as the bride of Christ. Though she was cloistered, many sought out her spiritual advice. Her influential writings, based on revelations, emphasize the Passion and the Sacred Heart.

26. Vision of God as Bleeding Pelican

My Lord, what would You teach me by this vision?

"I wish that you would consider the overflowing love that obliges Me to present you with such a gift; for after having thus given Myself, I would rather remain dead in the tomb, so to speak, than deprive a soul who loves Me of the fruit of My liberality. Consider also, that even as the blood that comes from the heart of the pelican gives life to its little ones, so also the soul whom I nourish with the divine Food I present to it receives a life that will never end."

27. God Compassionates Our Weakness

Lord, how is it that Your immaculate Body, in which You never had anything to reprove, compels You to compassionate our many weaknesses?

He replied: "... Has not My apostle said, 'It behooved him in all things to be made like his brethren, that he might be able to succor those who are tempted'? (See Heb 2:18.) This eye of My beloved, which pierces My heart, is the confidence that she ought to have in Me, because I know, I am able, and I am willing to assist her faithfully in all her miseries. And this confidence has such power over My goodness, that it is not possible for Me to abandon her."

But, Lord, if this confidence is so great a gift that none can have it unless You bestow it, how are those at fault who are deprived of it?

He replied: "Each can overcome his diffidence, in some degree, by the testimony of Scripture, and say, if not with his whole heart at least with his lips: 'If I should be cast into hell, you, O Lord, will deliver me' (Ps 16:10); and, 'Although he should kill me, I will trust him' (Job 13:15)."

28. Unseen Fruit of Prayers

[The Lord said:] "When a child returns from visiting an emperor who has enriched him with great possessions and much revenue, those who behold him in the weakness of childhood little imagine the treasures in his possession, although those who have been present are well aware how powerful and important his wealth will someday render him. Do not, therefore, be surprised if you do not see the fruits of your prayers with your bodily eyes, because I dispose of them, according to My eternal wisdom, to greater advantage. And know that the more you pray for anyone, the happier that person will become, because no prayer of faith can remain unfruitful, although we do not know what form its fruit will take."

29. Praying for a Sister

"Hear my petition for the person so often recommended to my prayers."

And immediately [Gertrude] beheld a stream, pure as crystal, flowing forth from the Heart of the Lord into the person for whom she prayed.

She then asked: "Lord, what will this person gain by this, since she does not see it flowing into her?"

He replied: "When a physician gives a draught to a sick man, those who are present do not see that person recover health the moment he takes the remedy, nor does the sick person feel cured; nevertheless, the physician knows well the value of the remedy, and how salutary it will prove to the patient."

"But why, Lord, don't you deliver her from the ill-regulated habits and the other defects from which I have implored you so many times to deliver her?"

He replied: "It is said of Me, when I was in my childhood, that I 'advanced in wisdom, and in age, and in grace with God and man' (Lk 2:52). So will this person advance from hour to hour, changing her faults into virtues; and I will deliver her from all the infirmities of nature."

30. Praying Against Inclement Weather

O charitable Lord, how can You so long resist the desires of so many people, since I, who am so unworthy of Your goodness, have often obtained much more considerable favors merely by having confidence in You?

"Why be surprised," replied our Lord, "that a father should allow his son to ask him repeatedly for a crown, if he set aside a hundred marks of gold for him each time the request was made? Neither should you be surprised if I defer answering your petition; because each time that you implore My aid by the least word, or even in thought, I prepare a recompense for you in eternity of infinitely greater value than a hundred marks of gold."

31. O Burning Furnace

I beheld my soul, as if it were wax softened by the fire, impressed like a seal upon the bosom of the Lord. Immediately I beheld it surrounding and partly drawn into this treasure house, where the ever-peaceful Trinity abides corporally in the plenitude of the Divinity and resplendent with its glorious impression.

O ardent fire of my God, which contains, produces, and imprints those living ardors that attract the humid waters of my soul and dry up the torrents of earthly delights and that afterward soften my hard self-opinionatedness, which time has hardened so exceedingly! O consuming fire, which even amid ardent flames imparts sweetness and peace to the soul! In You, and in none other, do we receive this grace of being reformed to the image and likeness in which we were created. O burning furnace, in which we enjoy the true vision of peace, which tries and purifies the gold of the elect, and leads the soul to seek eagerly for its highest good, even Yourself, in Your eternal truth!

32. My Beloved Daughter

It seems to me that I can truly say to You now, "Behold! My beloved Lord! Not only my inmost soul, but every part of my body, is moved toward You!"

"I know and feel it perfectly," replied our Lord, "because these graces have flowed from Me and returned to Me. But as for you, who are held captive in the chains of mortality, you can never understand all the reciprocal sweetness that My Divinity feels toward you. Know, however, that this movement of grace glorifies you, as My body was glorified on Mount Tabor, in the presence of My three beloved disciples; so that I can say of you, in the sweetness of My charity: 'This is my beloved daughter, in whom I am well pleased.' For it is the property of this grace to communicate to the body as well as to the mind a marvelous glory and brightness."

33. God, You Are…

You are the Life of my soul! May all the desires of my heart be united to You by Your burning love! May they languish and die whenever they turn to any object apart from You; for You are the beauty of all colors, the sweetness of all taste, the fragrance of all odors, the harmony of all sounds, the charm of all embraces! In You is the voluptuousness of delight; from You flows a torrent of love; to You are all drawn by Your powerful attractions. And by You all receive the sweet influences of love! You are the overflowing abyss of the Divinity! O King, greater than all kings! Supreme Emperor, sovereign Prince, peaceful Ruler! Faithful Protector! You are the vivifying gem of human nobility with the noblest sentiments! You are a Worker full of skill; a Master full of mercy; a Counselor full of wisdom, a Defender full of kindness; a Friend most faithful!

34. God, You Are… (continued)

You are the sweet savor of all delights! O gentle Caresser, whose touch imparts healing! O ardent Lover, sweet and chaste Spouse! You are the Spring-Flower of unchanging beauty! O loving Brother, beautiful Youth, joyful Companion, liberal Host, careful Administrator! I prefer You to every creature. For You I renounce all pleasures; for You I seek all adversity; and in all this I desire only Your glory. My heart and lips testify that You are the quickener of all good. I unite, by the merit of Your love, the fervor of my devotions to the virtue of Your prayers, so that by the power of this divine union I may be raised to the highest perfection, and all rebellious movements may be calmed within me.

35. Prayer Approaching Death

Accept my grief for the numerous offenses I have committed against the nobleness of Your divine goodness. I offer it to You, with all the gratitude and all the reverence that You have enabled me, for all in heaven, on earth, and in the deep, through the merit of Your beloved Son, and by the power of the Holy Spirit....

I give thanks with all my might, O Lord, my Creator and re-Creator, to Your infinite mercy, that, from the abyss of Your overflowing goodness, You have made known to me that whosoever shall remember me ... for Your glory, either by praying for sinners, or by giving thanks for the elect, or by any other good works, shall not leave this world until You have granted him the grace to become pleasing to You, and so order his heart that You may find joy and pleasure therein. For which may eternal praise be given to You, which shall return without ceasing to the uncreated love from which it proceeded!

Mechtild
of Magdeburg
1212-1282

Mechtild, born in Germany, joined and led a group of beguines, single women who lived in community and took vows of poverty and chastity but were not nuns. Her writing, *The Flowing Light of the Godhead,* and her vocal criticism of the clergy drew great opposition. As an older woman she joined the notable Helfta Cistercian Convent, home of Gertrude the Great.

36. Seven Kinds of Love for God

True love of God has seven approaches.
Cheerful love leads the way.
Fearing love takes on the task.
Strong love can accomplish much.
Loving love receives no honor.
Wise love has knowledge.
Free love lives without heartache.
Powerful love is forever happy.

37. The Beam of the Godhead

There also four beams [of light] were visible that shot forth continuously from the crossbow of the Holy Trinity from the divine throne through the nine choirs. There is no one, however rich or poor, whom the beam does not strike lovingly. The beam of the Godhead shoots incomprehensible light through them. Loving humanity greets them in fraternal company. The Holy Spirit touches them with the flood of the marvelous abundance of eternal bliss. Undivided God feeds them with the shimmer of His glorious countenance and fills them with the joyful breath of His flowing mouth. They glide effortlessly, as birds in the air do when not moving their wings, and they fly wherever they want, body and soul, and yet they remain separate in their own order.

> The Godhead rings,
> Humanity sings,
> The Holy Spirit plucks the harp of the heavens
> So that all strings resound
> That are strung in love.

38. Soulful Garments

You shine into my soul
Like the sun against gold.
When I may rest in You, Lord,
My joy is rich.
You clothe Yourself with my soul
And You are her most intimate garment.
That there must be a parting between them—
Never have I experienced greater heartache!
If You were to love me more intensely,
I would certainly pass away
To where I could love You as I wish unceasingly.
Now I have sung to You
And yet to no avail.
Were You to sing to me,
I would have to succeed.

39. God's Singing Response in the Soul

[God said:] When I shine, you shall glow.
When I flow, you shall become wet.
When you sigh, you draw My divine heart into you.
When you weep in longing for Me, I take you in My arms.
But when you love, we two become one being.
And when we two are one being,
Then we can never be parted.
Rather, a blissful abiding
Prevails between us.
[My soul replied:] Lord, then I shall persevere in hunger and
    thirst
In pursuing and in pleasure
Till that playful hour
When from Your divine mouth
The chosen words shall flow
That are heard by no one
But the soul alone
That has stripped itself of the earth
And puts her ear next to Your mouth.
She, indeed, grasps the treasure of love!

40. A Good Person's Prayer

That prayer has great power
Which a person undertakes with all his might.
It makes a bitter heart sweet
A sad heart happy
A poor heart rich
A foolish heart wise
A faltering heart bold
A weak heart strong
A blind heart seeing
A cold soul burning.
It draws great God down into a small heart.
It drives the hungry soul up to God's fullness.
It brings together two lovers, God and the soul, to a place
  of bliss.
There they talk much of love.
O woe! That I, unhappy sack of misery, cannot die there!

Hadewijch
Thirteenth Century

Little is known of the life of Hadewijch, a well-read leader of a community of Dutch beguines, dedicated to a spiritual life and acts of charity. Her Trinitarian writings, which include some of the earliest Dutch lyrical poems, were not discovered until the late nineteenth century. A visionary, she saw herself as the spouse of love. The following selections are from her letters.

41. Learn to Contemplate What God Is

Learn to contemplate what God is: how He is Truth (Jn 14:6), present to all things; and Goodness, overflowing with all wealth; and Totality, replete with all virtues. It is for these three names that the *Sanctus* is sung three times in heaven (Is 6:3), for they comprehend in their one essence all the virtues, whatever may be their particular works from their three distinct attributes.

See how God has protected you with fatherliness, and what He has given you, and what He has promised you. Behold how sublime is the love of the Three Persons for one another, and show your gratitude to God through love. Do this, if you wish to contemplate what God is and to work in Him, in His radiance, with fruition in glory and manifestation in radiance, in order to enlighten all things or to leave them in darkness, according to what they are.

42. Fall Deep Into Love

O beloved, why has not Love sufficiently overwhelmed you and engulfed you in her abyss? Alas! When Love is so sweet, why do you not fall deep into her? And why do you not touch God deeply enough in the abyss of His Nature, which is so unfathomable? Sweet love, give yourself for Love's sake fully to God in love....

O dear love, do not be remiss in virtue, no matter what the suffering! You busy yourself unduly with many things, and so many of them are not suited to you. You waste too much time with your energy, throwing yourself headlong into the things that cross your path. I could not persuade you to observe moderation in this. When you want to do something, you always plunge into it as if you could pay heed to nothing else. It pleases me that you comfort and help your friends, yes, the more the better—provided you and they remain in peace.

43. The Weightiest Command

For it seems to me that the commandment of love that God spoke to Moses is the weightiest I know in Scripture: *You shall love your Lord your God with all your heart, with all your soul, and with all your strength* (Dt 6:5). When He had said this, He continued: These words you shall never forget, sleeping or waking. If you sleep, you must dream of them; if you are awake, you must think of them, and recite them, and carry them into effect. These words you shall write on the threshold, and on the lintel, and on the wall, and in all the places where you shall be, that you may not forget what you must do there (cf. Dt 6:6-9).

In other words, God Himself commands that we nevermore forget Love, either sleeping or waking, in any manner, with all that we are, with heart, with soul, with mind, with strength, and with our thoughts. He gave this commandment to Moses and in the Gospel (Mt 22:37; Mk 12:30; Lk 10:27), that in this way we should live wholly for Love. Woe indeed! How dare we then give Love short measure in anything? Alas, is it not fearful robbery (Is 61:8) that we spare anything for Love, or hold back anything? Alas! Think about this, and work without neglect to promote Love above all things.

44. Be Satisfied With Nothing Less

Be satisfied with nothing less than Love. Give reason its time, and always observe where you heed it too little and where enough. And do not let yourself be stopped by any pleasure through which your reason may be the loser. What I mean by "your reason" is that you must keep your insight ever vigilant in the use of discernment. Never must any difficulty hinder you from serving people, be they insignificant or important, sick or healthy. And the sicker they are, and the fewer friends they have, the more readily must you serve them. And always bear with aliens willingly. As for all who slander you, contradict them not. And be desirous to associate with all who scorn you, for they make the way of Love broader for you.

Leave not anyone in need out of spite. And never fail to ask about any wise teaching you are ignorant of, out of spite or shame that you do not know it. For you are bound before God to acquire a knowledge of all the virtues and to learn them by exertion, questioning, study, and earnest purpose.

45. People Wish for Consolations...

Nowadays this is the way everyone loves himself; people wish to live with God in consolations and repose, in wealth and power, and to share the fruition of His glory. We all indeed wish to be God with God, but God knows there are few of us who want to live as men with His Humanity, or want to carry His cross with Him, or want to hang on the cross with Him and pay humanity's debt to the full. Indeed we can rightly discern this as regards ourselves, in that we are so little able to hold out against suffering in all respects. An unexpected sorrow, though slight, goes to our heart; or a slander, or a lie that people tell about us; or someone's robbing us of our honor, or our rest or of our own will: How quickly and deeply any of this wounds us all! And we know so well what we want or do not want, there are so many things and kinds of things for which we have an attraction or an aversion: now alike, now different; now sweetness, now bitterness; now here, now there; now off, now on; and as regards everything, we are so ready to provide for ourselves where any repose for us is in sight!

Blessed
Margaret Ebner
1291-1351

From a prominent German family, at fifteen Margaret entered a Dominican convent. For nearly forty years she suffered traumatic ailments, which she identified with Christ's Passion. She experienced a "binding silence"—an inability to speak—often followed by uncontrollable speaking of Jesus' name and exquisite ecstasies. Through correspondence Margaret was connected to a significant group of male mystics, including John Tauler, through whom she well knew Mechtild's *Flowing Light of the Godhead*.

46. Many Words Similar to These

[The Lord said,] "If I am your love, then you are My love. If your delight is in Me, then I am in you with all My power and I will never part from your soul and your heart until your soul is in eternal life." I said, "Jesus, You are pure Truth, teach me truth." He answered, "I am the Truth that lives in you and works through you and will accomplish even more through you to My eternal honor." And I said, "Jesus, You are boundless Mercy, have mercy on me and come to my aid." And He said, "I have helped you and I will never withdraw My help from you." …

… "My strong love is your consolation, My sweet grace is your strength, My divine delight is your satisfaction, My divine mercy is your help, and My pure truth your teaching." And He said many words similar to these, but I can no longer remember them.

47. I Am Your Love

[The Lord said,] "I have given Myself to you and will never withdraw Myself from you. It is I alone, the true God, who should possess your heart. All your delight is in Me and all My delight is in your soul and in your heart. You are My love as I am your love. You do not understand that it is My pure love from which all this comes to you. Suffer Me for the sake of My love, because I cannot do without your acceptance of it. It is I alone, the pure Truth, who lives in you and works through you, and I have surrounded you with My mercy. Rejoice that the true God lives in you and that My goodness will never forsake you in time or in eternity. I am your sweet delight on earth and you are My joy in heaven. Compelled by My very love, I have chosen you for Myself in order to accomplish in you yet more for My eternal honor here and hereafter. It is I alone, your Lord and your God and your only Love, who accomplishes great things in you."

48. Dreaming During Matin Prayers

I fell asleep and … saw many people behind the choir stalls dressed in white. I wanted to sprinkle them with water from the font in order to see what they would do. Then they all came running over to me with great joy. I was happy and thought I would say, "Jesus Christ," to see how they would respond to it. And so I said, "Jesus Christ." At that they fell down on their knees with great desire and repeated, "Jesus Christ." From that I gained such great grace and joy that I began to sing the sweet Name of Jesus Christ and they sang with me. And I said, "We should dance." Then they answered, "We should dance and eat and drink with one another." Then it seemed to me as if one of the sisters came and opened up the door to choir. That was disappointing to me and to them because we were interrupted and I would gladly have stayed with them always. Then I awoke and all my sickness had ceased and I was made glad and received great desire to know who they were. I asked my Child Jesus about them. He said, "To you has been shown the joy and the love that reign in heaven."

49. Accomplish in Us the Sweetest Works

Give us, my Lord, constant attentiveness to ourselves in Your heartfelt love and a powerful sign of victory over all evil. And give us, my Lord, the truth in which we will know and love You. Give us, too, Your boundless mercy by which we grow refined and purified from all our sins so that we appear as pure before the luminous mirror of Your divine face as when our soul was poured into our body and our body was lifted up from the waters of baptism.

I ask You, my Lord Jesus Christ, by Your perfect grace, to help us always to be guided by Your will, be good or ill done to us, so that Your powerful might may bind us and Your sweet love compel us such that we may have no mere natural life in us, but may You, Jesus Christ, live in us with all Your grace; and may we live for You alone in truth. And I ask You to accomplish in us powerfully the sweetest works that You have done out of inner delight in Your chosen friends, until we perceive what right love for You is.

50. The True Light of Your Pure Life

My Lord, may Your glorified, grace-filled humanity, Jesus Christ, be my innermost strength, a purification of my whole life, and an enlightening of all my senses to recognize the real and only truth. My surest way to You, my Lord, on the way of real truth must be for me the true light of Your pure life of thirty-three years on earth: Your humble deeds, Your gentle course of life, Your powerful suffering, Your love-filled death, Your true words.

My Lord, give me a sweet assurance of salvation in the fullness of Your grace, a loving end in right disposition, an eternal enjoyment of nothing but Your love, where You alone, my Lord, are Lord and no one else, and where Your honor is our eternal food and Your power our eternal joy; where Your clear appearance is our eternal guide and where all sadness has an end and all joy is assured by the source of living water. Whence does it flow? From the Father's heart, the Eternal Word, enclosed for love of us in the Virgin's womb in nothing but purity.

Saint Bridget of Sweden
1302-1373

Bridget, a Third-Order Franciscan, dedicated her life to prayer, pilgrimage, and service to the poor. She also mothered eight children. Widowed, she founded the "Bridgettine" order. As one of Sweden's wealthiest daughters, she had access to kings, queens, and popes, whom she chastised like a prophet. Her *Revelations* were widely distributed and read.

51. When Criticized for Being a "Fanciful Dreamer"

Blessed be that good priest who knows me and my faults so well. He speaks most truly when he says that I am weak in my understanding and judgment, for I have loved creatures more than God. In the future, I will love nothing but my Maker and my Lord and aim only at pleasing Him, so shall I come to a right mind, pleasing God and not the world. I humbly beg the prayers of that priest and promise to pray for him in return.

52. Why Me?

O King of Glory, my Lord and my God, I, who am as the vilest worm before You, ask how it is that You have chosen for Your service one who has spent her strength in sinning against You. O my Lord, Son of the Virgin, why have You stooped to make Your abode with a poor and wretched widow, empty of good works and careless in the practice of virtue? Be not angry with me, Jesus, my sweetest Lord, that I ask You this, for indeed no one can wonder at You who does whatever pleases You. But well may I wonder about myself, who has so grievously offended You and so little amended my faults.

Jesus answered, "I do what I will with what is Mine, and because you are Mine, wonder not at what befalls you by My will. Only be constant, courageous in suffering, and prompt to do whatever I require of you, for I can give you all that you need."

53. The Divine Bridegroom Speaks

As My head was pierced with thorns and bowed upon the cross for you, so must yours be bowed in humility. As My eyes were full of tears and blood, yours must be turned away from things that please them. My ears were filled with insults and reproaches; yours must be closed to words of vanity. My mouth drank a bitter draught and tasted no sweetness; yours must be closed to all words but such as are good and salutary. My hands were stretched out and pierced with nails; so must your works, which are represented by the hands, be for the poor and the fulfilling of My commandments. My feet, that is, the affections that are to lead you to Me, must be crucified to the sinful joys of this world. And as I suffered in all My limbs, so must all yours be ready to give Me obedience. It is meet that the bride should be wearied, like her Bridegroom, with labor and suffering, so shall she rest more lovingly with Him.

54. The Divine Teacher Speaks

I have taught you these three things, and by them you may know the good Spirit. I have taught you to honor God your Maker, who has given you all that you have. I have taught you to hold the right faith, that is, to believe that nothing exists or can exist but by God. I have taught you to practice a prudent temperance in all created things. By the opposite of these three teachings you may know the bad spirit. He tries to make you seek to be praised and to be proud of the graces you have received. He tempts you to unfaithfulness and self-indulgence. Sometimes he deceives you by an appearance of good. For this cause I have commanded you always to examine your conscience honestly and to consult wise and spiritual counsel. Never doubt that God's good Spirit is with you so long as you desire God alone.... I alone can give you this desire, and with it, it is impossible for Satan to come near you.... It may sometimes happen that the devil has power over the bodies of the good; sometimes, too, he darkens their conscience, but he can never have dominion over the souls of those who believe and love Me.

55. The Book of Questions

Why, O Judge, don't You let Your glory appear in this life before the human eye, so that people may desire it more fervently? And if the devils are so monstrous and hideous, why don't You let them be made visible, so that no one should follow them?

"My glory is unspeakable, and its beauty and excellence incomparable. If it were made visible as it is, mortal bodies would become weak and powerless, as happened to those who saw My glory on the Mount. They would also be incapable of work because of the soul's rapture. But as no one can enter heaven who does not practice works of charity, so that faith may have its reward and the body be strengthened for work,

My glory is hidden for a time, so that it may be more abundantly and blessedly contemplated in eternity, through the exercise of desire and faith in this world. As to why the devils do not appear visibly, if their frightful deformity could be seen, the soul of the beholder would lose its powers through horror at the sight.... So the hideousness of the devils is concealed and their malice restrained, that the soul may be strong, his understanding sound, and his heart full of the joy of My love."

56. Prayer When Called to Found an Order

O incorporeal Power! How great is Your condescension! I know most certainly that You refuse mercy to no one, however unworthy, who asks it of You with true humility and a firm purpose of abandoning his sins. Bear witness that I, through Your grace, have the will to do Your will. You know that if it were possible to increase Your joy and blessedness by bearing in my body all kinds of sickness, pain, poverty, and affliction, even eternal punishment in my soul, I would rather suffer these torments in body and soul than to have Your bliss be lessened. O God, who has created me and redeemed me with Your precious blood, if You see me lacking in faith, hope, and charity, by Your almighty grace supply what is needed. You dwell in my inmost heart. You are the Beloved of my soul. Unworthy as I am to be visited and consoled by Your blessed Spirit, yet I put myself under Your almighty protection to do with me as You please.... I, the most worthless of creatures, am among Your faithful servants as a little ant among mighty camels carrying great burdens for the use and glory of their lord. How will it be possible for the pope to believe that you … have stooped down to do such great things to such a miserable ant?

57. Our Lady Speaks

The heart of my Son is sweet as honey and pure as a crystal fountain. From it all virtue and goodness flow, as from their source. It is sweeter and more beautiful than all things, for what can be so great a joy to man as to think of the exceeding great love of Jesus as shown in His labors and teaching, His sweetness and patience in the work of their redemption: His love does not pass away like running water, but is faithful, lasting, and all embracing, so that a sinner, though standing at the very gate of hell, who cried there for help, resolving to amend, would be saved.

58. Saint Francis Speaks

Welcome, my daughter! It is true that I bade you come to my cell to eat and drink with me. But I did not speak of this church. What I meant by my cell was the obedience I always observed so faithfully that I chose never to be without someone whose behests I was bound to obey.... The food that was my support and refreshment was to win my neighbor from the vanities of this life to serve God with all his heart. When this happened, my joy was the sweetest food I could taste. My drink was the delight I felt when the souls I converted loved God with all their strength, gave themselves to meditation and prayer, won others to a devout life, and practiced the love of holy poverty. My daughter, this was the drink that so gladdened my soul that I was disgusted with everything in this world. Go into this cell of mine, eat this food, and drink this drink—so shall you be eternally refreshed by God.

59. Mary's Rebuke to the Church

I am like the rainbow above the clouds, which seems to stoop down and touch the earth with both ends, for I stoop down to the dwellers on earth and touch both bad and good by my prayers—the good, that they may be faithful to the bidding of Holy Church, their Mother; the bad that they may not continue and grow worse in their sins. I now make known to those to whom my words are sent that from one part of the earth terrible clouds are rising up against the brightness of the rainbow. Most of the ministers of the Church are sunk in worldly pleasure, the love of money, pomp, and pride. Their sins rise up from the earth to heaven against my prayers as the dark clouds come over the sky's bright rainbow.... Such men ought to be put down instead of being exalted in the Church. But whosoever will do his part in strengthening its foundations, and desire to make the pavement even and to renovate the holy vineyard that God has planted and watered with His blood, he shall receive help from me, the Queen of heaven, and all the angelic host, in everything beyond his strength.... The vineyard I speak of is God's Holy Church, which needs renewing in humility and divine charity.

60. Near Death: The Comforter Speaks

What do these physicians say, my daughter? That you shall not die? They do not know what it is to die. To die is to be separated from God, to be hardened in sin, to refuse to cleanse the soul by penitent confession. He is dead who has no faith in God, no love for his Maker. But he does not die who always fears God, keeps his conscience pure by frequent confession, and desires to be united to his Lord. The God of nature, who can alter the course of nature, and to whom alone it belongs to support life, He bids you know that there is no virtue or saving for your life in any medicine. You have no need of it, for a short time needs little nourishment.

Blessed Julian
of Norwich
1342-1423

At age thirty Julian received sixteen visions, which she recorded in the first known book written by a woman in English, *Revelations of Divine Love*. An anchoress, she lived alone in a "cell" attached to the church in Norwich. Without leaving her home, she received visitors asking for spiritual direction.

61. Heavenly Bliss

In this revelation my understanding was lifted up into heaven, where I saw our Lord as a lord in His own house who has called all His dear-worthy servants and friends to a stately feast. Then I saw the Lord take no place in His own house, but I saw Him royally reign in His house, fulfilling it with joy and mirth, Himself endlessly to gladden and to solace His dear-worthy friends, full homely and full courteously, with marvelous melody of endless love, in His own fair blessed countenance. This glorious countenance of the Godhead filled the heavens with joy and bliss.

62. Seek the Lord

The continual seeking of the soul pleases God full greatly, for the soul can do no more than seek, suffer, and trust. And this is wrought in the soul by the Holy Ghost. Those who clearly find God do so of His special grace, when it is His will. The seeking, with faith, hope, and charity, pleases our Lord, and the finding pleases the soul and fills it with joy. And so my understanding learned that seeking is as good as beholding....

It is God's will that we have three things in our seeking: The first is that we seek earnestly and diligently, without sloth, and, as it may be through His grace, without unreasonable heaviness and vain sorrow. The second is that we abide Him steadfastly for His love, without murmuring and striving against Him, to our life's end, for life shall last but awhile. The third is that we trust in Him mightily of full assured faith. It is His will that we know that He shall appear suddenly and blissfully to all who love Him. His working is secret, but He wills to be perceived, and His appearing shall be swiftly sudden. He wills to be trusted. For He is full gracious and homely. Blessed may He be!

63. Some Days Up, Some Days Down

It is speedful to some souls to feel on this wise: Sometimes to be in comfort, and sometimes to fail and to be left to themselves. God wills that we know that He keeps us even alike secure in woe and in weal. And for profit of the soul, a person is sometimes left to himself, although sin is not always the cause. For in this time [of woe] I sinned not so as to be left to myself—for it was so sudden. Nor did I deserve to have this blessed feeling [of comfort]. But freely our Lord gives when He will, and suffers us sometimes to be in woe. And both is one love. For it is God's will that we hold us in His comfort with all our might, for bliss is everlasting, but pain is passing and shall be brought to naught for them that shall be saved. Therefore it is not God's will that we follow the feelings of pain, being sorrowful and mournful for them, but that we suddenly pass over and hold us in endless enjoyment.

64. Large Prayers, Large Trust

This is our Lord's will, that our prayer and our trust be both alike large. For if we trust not as much as we pray, we do not full worship to our Lord in our prayer, and also we tarry and pain our self. The cause is, as I believe, that we know not truly that our Lord is the Ground on whom our prayer springs, and also that we know not that it is given us by the grace of His love. For if we knew this, it would make us to trust to have all that we desire of our Lord's gift. For I am sure that no one asks mercy and grace with true meaning, unless mercy and grace be first given to him.

Sometimes it seems we have prayed long, and yet we think that we have not our asking. Here we should not be in heaviness. For I am sure our Lord's meaning is that we wait for a better time or more grace or a better gift.

He wills that we have true knowing that He is Being. In this knowing He wills that our understanding be grounded, with all our might and all our intent and all our meaning. In this ground He wills that we take our place and our dwelling.

65. All-Mighty, All-Wisdom, All-Goodness

I saw no difference between God and our Substance, but, as it were, all God. And yet my understanding took that our Substance is in God; that is, that God is God and our Substance is a creature in God. For the almighty Truth of the Trinity is our Father, for He made us and keeps us in Him. And the deep Wisdom of the Trinity is our Mother, in whom we are all enclosed. The high Goodness of the Trinity is our Lord, and in Him we are enclosed, and He in us. We are enclosed in the Father, and we are enclosed in the Son, and we are enclosed in the Holy Ghost. And the Father is enclosed in us, and the Son is enclosed in us, and the Holy Ghost is enclosed in us: All-Mightiness, All-Wisdom, All-Goodness: one God, one Lord.

66. The Salvation of a Child

The mother may suffer the child to fall sometimes, and to be hurt in diverse manners for its own profit, but she may never suffer that any manner of peril come to the child, for love. And though our earthly mother may suffer her child to perish, our heavenly Mother, Jesus, may not suffer us that are His children to perish, for He is All-Mighty, All-Wisdom, and All-Love, and so is none but He, blessed may He be!…

He wills that we take ourselves mightily to the faith of Holy Church and find there our dear-worthy Mother, in solace of true understanding, with all the blessed common. For one single person may often be broken, or seem so to himself, but the whole Church body was never broken, nor ever shall be, without end. And therefore a sure thing it is, good and gracious, to will meekly and mightily to be fastened and oned to our Mother, Holy Church, that is, Christ Jesus. For the food of mercy that is His dear-worthy blood and precious water is plenteous to make us fair and clean.… He in all this working uses the office of a kind nurse that has naught else to do but to give heed about the salvation of her child.

67. All Shall Be Well

He said in the last word, with full true secureness, meaning us all: *Thou shalt not be overcome.* All this teaching in this true comfort, it is general, to all my even-Christians, as I said before, and it is God's will.

This word, *Thou shalt not be overcome,* was said full decisively and full mightily, for assuredness and comfort against all tribulations that may come. He said not, *Thou shalt not be tempted, thou shalt not be travailed, thou shalt not be afflicted.* But he said, *Thou shalt not be overcome.* God willed that we take heed to these words, and that we be ever strong in sure trust, in weal and woe. For He loves and enjoys us, and so wills He that we love and enjoy Him and mightily trust in Him. And *all shall be well.*

68. "I It Am"

For all our life is in three: in the first we have our Being, in the second we have our Increasing, and in the third we have our Fulfilling. The first is Nature, the second is Mercy, and the third is Grace....

As verily as God is our Father, so verily God is our Mother. And that showed He in all, and especially in these sweet words, where He said: *I it am.* That is, *I it am, the Might and the Goodness of the Fatherhood; I it am, the Wisdom of the Motherhood; I it am, the Light and the Grace that is all blessed Love; I it am, the Trinity; I it am, the Unity; I am the sovereign Goodness of all manner of things. I am that makes you to love. I am that makes you to long. I it am, the endless fulfilling of all true desires.*

For there the soul is highest, noblest, and worthiest, where it is lowest, meekest, and mildest. And out of this substantial Ground we have all our virtues in our Sense—part by gift of Nature, by helping and speeding of Mercy and Grace, without which we may not profit.

69. Marvel at the Greatness

We shall see the cause of all things that He has done, and evermore we shall see the cause of all things that He has permitted. And the bliss and the fulfilling shall be so deep and so high that, for wonder and marvel, all creatures shall have for God so great reverent dread, overpassing that which has been seen and felt before, that the pillars of heaven shall tremble and quake. But this manner of trembling and dread shall have no pain, but it belongs to the worthy might of God thus to be beheld by His creatures, in great dread trembling and quaking for meekness of joy, marveling at the greatness of God the Maker and at the littleness of all that is made. For the beholding of this makes the creature marvelously meek and mild.

Wherefore God wills—and also it belongs to us, both in nature and grace—that we attend and know of this, desiring this sight and this working. For it leads us in the right way and keeps us in true life and ones us to God. And as good as God is, so great He is, and as much as it belongs to His goodness to be loved, so it belongs to His greatness to be dreaded.

70. The Wisest Course...

... is for a creature to follow the will and counsel of his highest sovereign Friend. This blessed Friend is Jesus, and it is His will and counsel that we hold ourselves with Him and fasten ourselves to Him homely, evermore, in whatever state we be, for whether we be foul or clean, we are all one in His loving. For weal or woe, He wills never we flee from Him. But because of the changeability in our self, we often fall into sin. Then we have this doubting dread stirred up by our enemy and by our own folly and blindness, which say: *You see, you are a wretched sinner and unfaithful, for you keep not the command; you often promised our Lord that you would do better, and anon after you fall again into the same, especially into sloth and losing of time.* (For that is the beginning of sin, in my view....) And this makes us dread to appear before our courteous Lord. It is our enemy that would put us aback with his false dread because of our wretchedness, through pain that he threatens us with. For it is his meaning to make us so heavy and weary in this, that we should let out of mind the fair, blissful beholding of our everlasting Friend.

Saint Catherine of Siena
1347-1380

As a lay Dominican, Catherine dedicated herself to helping the sick and poor and serving as a peacemaker in a deeply divided European Church. Suffering the wounds of the stigmata, she also knew great ecstasies, through which she "received" her major writings. The following selections are from this dictated *Dialogue*. (Except in the prayers, the voice is that of God.) Catherine has been declared a Doctor of the Church.

71. Prayer

Clothe me, clothe me with Yourself, O eternal Truth, that I may run my mortal course with true obedience and the light of holy faith, with which light I feel that my soul is about to become inebriated afresh.

72. Walk Over the Bridge

First I gave you the Bridge of My Son living and conversing in very deed among men. When He, the living Bridge, left you, there remained the Bridge and the road of His doctrine, as has been said, His doctrine being joined with My power and with His wisdom and with the mercy of the Holy Spirit. This power of Mine gives the virtue of fortitude to whomever follows this road; wisdom gives him light, so that, in this road, he may recognize the truth; and the Holy Spirit gives him love, which consumes and takes away all sensual love out of the soul, leaving there only the love of virtue. Thus, in both His life and through His doctrine, [Jesus] is the Way, the Truth, and the Life—the Bridge that leads you to the height of heaven....

Walk over the Bridge and not underneath it, because underneath is not the way of truth, but the way of falsehood, by which walk the wicked. These are those sinners for whom I beg you to pray to Me, and for whom I also ask your tears and sweat, that they may receive mercy from Me.

73. Blinded by Self-Love

The devil invites people to the water of death, that is, to that which he has, and, blinding them with the pleasures and conditions of the world, he catches them with the hook of pleasure, under the pretense of good; in no other way could he catch them, for they would not allow themselves to be caught if they saw that no good or pleasure to themselves were to be obtained thereby. For the soul, by its nature, always relishes good, though it is true that the soul, blinded by self-love, does not know and discern what is true good and of profit to the soul and to the body. Therefore, the devil, seeing them blinded by self-love, iniquitously places before them diverse and various delights, colored so as to have the appearance of some benefit or good. And he gives to everyone according to his condition and those principal vices to which he sees him to be most disposed—of one kind to the secular, of another to the religious, and others to prelates and noblemen, according to their different conditions. I have told you this because I now speak of those who drown themselves in the river, and who care for nothing but themselves.

74. They Do Not Have What They Long For

Love always brings suffering if what a person has identified with is lost. These souls in one way or another have identified with the earth in their love, and so they have in fact become earth themselves. Some have identified with their wealth, some with their status, some with their children. Some lose Me in their slavery to creatures. Some in their great indecency make brute beasts of their bodies. And so in one way and another they hunger for and feed on earth. They would like to be stable but are not. Indeed they are as passing as the wind, for either they themselves fail through death or My will deprives them of the very things they loved. They suffer unbearable pain in their loss. And the more disordered their love in possessing, the greater is their grief in loss. Had they held these things as lent to them rather than as their own, they could let them go without pain. They suffer because they do not have what they long for. For, as I told you, the world cannot satisfy them, and not being satisfied, they suffer.

75. Love and Consolation

Some become faithful servants, serving Me with fidelity not for fear of punishment, but rather with love. This love is imperfect if they serve Me with a view to their own profit or the delight and pleasure they find in Me. What proves this love imperfect? The withdrawal of the consolations they found in Me, and the insufficiency and short duration of their love for their neighbor, which grows weak by degrees and often disappears. Their love toward Me grows weak when I occasionally withdraw My consolation from their minds and allow them to fall into battles and perplexities. I do this so that they, coming to perfect self-knowledge, may know that of themselves they are nothing and have no grace; so that in time of battle they would fly to Me, as their Benefactor, seeking Me alone, with true humility. This is why I withdraw from them consolation but not grace.... Such a soul, loving imperfectly, has not yet unwound the bandage of spiritual self-love, for, had she unwound it, she would see that, in truth, everything proceeds from Me, that no leaf of a tree falls to the ground without My providence, and that what I give and promise to My creatures, I give and promise for their sanctification.

76. Love of Neighbor

If a man carries away the vessel that he has filled at the fountain and then drinks of it, the vessel becomes empty, but if he keeps his vessel standing in the fountain while he drinks, it always remains full. So the love of the neighbor, whether spiritual or temporal, should be drunk in Me, without any self-regarding considerations.

I require that you should love Me with the same love with which I love you. This indeed you cannot do, because I loved you without being loved. All the love that you have for Me you owe to Me, so that it is not of grace that you love Me, but because you ought to do so. I love you of grace, and not because I owe you my love. Therefore to Me, in person, you cannot repay the love I require of you. I have placed you in the midst of your fellows, so you may do to them that which you cannot do to Me, that is, love your neighbor of free grace, without expecting any return from him. And what you do to him, I count as done to Me.

77. Freedom in Christ

Reprove yourself if ever the devil or your own short-sightedness should do you the disservice of making you want to force all My servants to walk by the same path you yourself follow, for this would be contrary to the teaching given you by My truth. It often happens, when many are going the way of great penance, that some people would like to make everyone go that very same way. And if everyone does not do so, they are displeased and scandalized because they think these others are not doing the right thing. But you see how deluded they are, because it often happens that those who seem to be doing wrong because they do less penance are actually better and more virtuous, even though they do not perform such great penances, than those who are doing the grumbling.

78. Visitation Linked to Virtue

This is the sign by which you can discern that gladness is indeed signaling a visitation from Me: If it is joined with virtue. This is truly a clear sign to show you what is delusion and what is not, which spiritual gladness comes from Me in truth and which comes from spiritual selfishness, that is, from love and affection for one's own consolation. The visitation that comes from Me is accompanied by gladness with love for virtue; that which comes from the devil brings merely the gladness, and when one takes a closer look, there is no more virtue than there was before. Such gladness comes only from love for one's own consolation.

I want you to know that not everyone is deluded by this gladness. It is only these imperfect souls who hanker after pleasure and consolation and are more concerned about my gift than about Me, the Giver. But there are others who are sincere and without any self-interest. These, afire as they are with love, look only to Me, the Giver, and not to the gift.

79. O Gentle Father …

O gentle Father, when the human race lay sick through the sin of Adam, you sent it a Physician, the gentle and amorous Word—Your Son. And now, when I was lying infirm with the sickness of negligence and much ignorance, You, most soothing and gentle Physician, eternal God, have given a soothing, sweet, and bitter medicine, that I may be cured and rise from my infirmity. You have soothed me because with Your love and gentleness You have manifested Yourself to me, Sweet above all prayer. Now I beg of You that You will do mercy to the world and to the Holy Church.…

Open the door of Your inestimable love, which You have given us through the door of Your Word. I know indeed that You open even before we can knock, for it is with the affection of love that You have given to Your servants, that they knock and cry to You, seeking Your honor and the salvation of souls. Give them then the Bread of Life, that is, the fruit of the blood of Your Son, which they ask of You for the praise and glory of Your name and the salvation of souls.

80. The Fire of God's Charity

Thanks, thanks to You, O eternal Father, for You have not despised me, the work of Your hands, nor turned Your face from me, nor despised my desires. You, the Light, have not regarded my darkness. You, true Life, have not regarded my living death. You, the Physician, have not been repelled by my grave infirmities. You, the eternal Purity, have not considered the many miseries of which I am full. You, the Infinite, have not overlooked that I am finite. You, who are Wisdom, have overlooked my folly. Your wisdom, Your goodness, Your mercy, Your infinite good, have overlooked these infinite evils and sins. Having known the truth through Your mercy, I have found Your charity and the love of my neighbor. What has constrained me? Not my virtues, but only Your charity. May that same charity constrain You to illuminate the eye of my intellect with the light of faith, so that I may know and understand the truth You have manifested to me. Grant that my memory may be capable of retaining Your benefits, that my will may burn in the fire of Your charity.

Saint Catherine
of Genoa
1447-1510

Catherine's aristocratic Italian family arranged her youthful marriage—to a difficult man. At age twenty-six, chronically depressed, she had a profound spiritual experience, overwhelmed with the love of God. From then on she devoted her life, despite at times great physical pain, to service to the poor, even taking charge of the hospital at Genoa. (Her husband also underwent a transforming conversion.)

81. Grace Abounds

Grace increases in proportion as one makes use of it. Hence it is evident that God gives us from day to day all that we need, no more and no less, and to each according to his condition and capacity. All this He does for the love and benefit of mankind, but because we are so cold and negligent in our endeavors, and because the instinct of the spirit is to arrive quickly at perfection, it seems as if grace were insufficient. Yet it is not so, and the fault is wholly ours, in not cooperating with the grace already received, which therefore ceases to increase.

O wretched one! How shall you be excused for failing to correspond with that great love and care which God has always bestowed and still bestows upon you? At the hour of death you will behold and know all this, and you will then be speechless through astonishment. Then the truth will be made plain and you will have no power to contradict it.

82. The Lord, Her Love, Said...

My daughter, observe these three rules: Never say I will or I will not. Never say mine, but always ours. Never excuse yourself, but always accuse yourself.

When you repeat the Our Father take always for your maxim, *Fiat vuluntas tua,* that is, may His will be done in everything that may happen to you, whether good or ill; from the Hail Mary take the word *Jesus,* and may it be implanted in your heart, and it will be a sweet guide and shield to you in all the necessities of life. And from the rest of Scripture take always for your support this word, *Love,* with which you will go on your way, direct, pure, light, watchful, quick, enlightened, without erring, yet without a guide or help from any creature; for love needs no support, being sufficient to do all things without fear; neither does love ever become weary, for even martyrdom is sweet to it. And, finally, this love will consume all the inclinations of the soul, and the desires of the body, for the things of this life.

83. God Is My Me

Although mankind is created for the possession of happiness, yet, having deviated from his true end, his nature has become deformed and is entirely repugnant to true beatitude. And on this account we are forced to submit to God this depraved nature of ours, which fills our understanding with so many occupations, and causes us to deviate from the true path, in order that He may entirely consume it until nothing remains there but Himself; otherwise the soul could never attain stability nor repose, for she was created for no other end.

Whenever God can do so, He attracts the free will of man by sweet allurements, and afterward disposes it in such a manner that all things may conduce to the annihilation of man's proper being. So that in God is my being, my *me*, my strength, my beatitude, my good, and my delight. I say *mine* at present because it is not possible to speak otherwise; but I do not mean by it any such thing as *me* or *mine*, or delight or good, or strength or stability, or beatitude.

84. The Dark Night of the Soul

When the time came that pleased God, He drew the Spirit so secretly and closely to Himself, that it held no communication with the soul nor the soul with the body, and both were left so bare and dry that it was hard for them to live at all, especially at the first, when they were passing from one extreme to the other, although God was secretly attracting them by little and little. At length what happened to the soul is like what happens to a bombshell—when the fire is applied, it explodes and loses both fire and powder. Thus the soul, having conceived the fire of pure, divine love, suddenly lost that which had before inflamed her, and, deprived of all sensibility, could never more return to it. The soul resembled a musical instrument which, while furnished with strings, sends forth sweet melody, but, being deprived of them, is silent. So she, who had hitherto, with the senses of both soul and body, discoursed such sweet music, now, bereft of these, remained stringless and mute.

85. God's Thread of Love

O soul, the true love you are striving to comprehend is seen only when I [God] have consumed the imperfections of many by every mode of human misery, both exterior and interior. As for that which cannot be seen, this is My mode of action: I let down into the heart the slender, golden thread of My hidden love, to which is attached a hook that enters the heart, and that person feels wounded but knows not by whom he is bound and taken. That person neither moves nor wishes to move, because his heart is drawn by Me, its object and its end, although he does not comprehend it; but it is I who hold the thread in My hand, and draw it ever closer with a love so penetrating and so subtle that the person is conquered and subdued and entirely taken out of himself.

… God, having taken this person into His own keeping and drawn him entirely to Himself, so enriches him with His favors that when he comes to die he finds himself drawn unconsciously by that thread of love into the divine abyss. Although man in this state appears a lifeless, lost, and abject thing, yet his life is hidden in God amid the treasures of eternal life.

86. If I Could Express ...

O Love, no words of mine can express the sweetness and delight with which You fill the heart. It remains enclosed within, and by speaking it is inflamed. Whoever hears or reads these words without the sentiment of love makes little account of them, and they pass by that person like the wind. But if I could express the joy, the pleasure, and the peace that it brings to the beloved heart, all who hear or read these words would surrender without resistance. For it is so adapted to the human heart that at its first touch it opens wide its door, although no one can receive this celestial gift till one is free from every other love. If the heart receives but the smallest drop, it so earnestly desires to increase it that it rates as nothing all the goods of this world. With this love, one conquers the evil habits that are a hindrance and in its strength one stands ever ready to perform great deeds.

87. O Love...

Because the soul is immortal and capable of greater love than it can feel in this life, on account of the weakness of the body, which does not allow the soul to support all that it desires, it remains ever craving, and in this life can never be fully satisfied.

O Love, You fill the heart, but You are so great that it cannot contain You; it remains filled but not satisfied. By the road of the heart You take possession of the entire being and permit none but Yourself to find entrance. With a strong bond You bind all the faculties of soul and body. O sweet servitude of love, which gives freedom and contentment in this life and eternal blessedness in the other!

O Love, Your bonds are so sweet and so strong that they bind angels and saints together and so firm and close that they are never broken. Those who are bound by this chain are so united that they have but one will and one aim. In this union there is no difference between rich and poor, between nation and nation; all contradiction is excluded, for by this love crooked things are made straight and difficulties reconciled.

88. Holy Conversation

Soul: Show me, O my Lord, if You please, how You work within by the secret love, taking someone captive, though that person not know how but only find himself a prisoner of love and greatly satisfied.

Lord: With My love I move the human heart and with that movement give light by which he sees that I am inspiring him to well-doing; in that light he ceases to do ill and struggles with his evil inclinations.

Soul: What is this movement and how does it begin in someone who knows not of its existence and asks not for it?

Lord: The pure, simple, and boundless love I bear toward all impels Me to grant one this grace, to knock at the heart, to see whether he will open and give Me entrance, so I may make My abode there and banish all things else.

Soul: And what is this grace?

Lord: It is an inspiration I send by means of a ray of love, with which I give also the instinct of love; it is impossible for him not to love, and although he knows not what he loves, he learns it by little and little....

89. Wounded With Love

Soul: What is the ray of love?

Lord: Behold the rays of the sun, which are so subtle and penetrating that human eyes cannot behold them without losing their sight. Such are the rays of My love that I send into human hearts and that deprive humans of all knowledge and all delight in worldly things.

Soul: And these rays, how do they enter into human hearts?

Lord: Like darts directed at this one and at that. They touch the heart in secret, inflame it, and make it heave with sighs. One knows not what he wishes, but finding himself wounded with love can give no account of his condition and remains lost in wonder.

Soul: And what is this dart?

Lord: It is a scintillation of love that I infuse into a being, which melts him as fire melts wax. I give him also the instinct to refer to Me all the love I infuse.

Soul: And what is this scintillation?

Lord: It is an inspiration sent by Me that sets on fire the human heart and so ardently and powerfully inflames it, that it can do nothing but love.

90. Purgatory

Consider gold: the more often it is melted, the more pure it becomes. Continue to melt it and every imperfection is destroyed. This is the effect of fire on all materials. The soul, however, cannot be annihilated in God, but in herself she can, and the longer her purification lasts, the more perfectly does she die to herself, until at length she remains purified in God.

When gold has been completely freed from dross, no fire, however great, has any further action on it, for nothing but its imperfections can be consumed. So it is with the divine fire in the soul. God retains her in these flames until every stain is burned away, and she is brought to the highest perfection of which she is capable, each soul in her own degree. And when this is accomplished, she rests wholly in God. Nothing of herself remains, and God is her entire being. When He has thus led her to Himself and purified her, nothing remains to be consumed. If when thus refined she should again approach the fire, she would feel no pain, for to her it has become the fire of divine love, which is life eternal and which nothing mars.

Saint Teresa of Avila
1515-1582

This Spanish nun who knew the heights of ecstasy was always drawn back to a life of service. Facing great opposition and hardship, she reformed her order, founding and overseeing the Discalced (Barefoot) Carmelites. She wrote extensively about prayer and the devout life, and has been named a Doctor of the Church. Several of the following selections draw on an extended "water" image used in her *Autobiography*.

91. The Garden of Prayer

One who commences prayer should imagine that for the delight of his Lord, he is starting to plant a garden in some very unfruitful soil, full of weeds. His Majesty must be asked to pull up the bad plants, and put good ones in their place. But we will suppose this is already done, when a soul has not only determined, but is resolved to make use of mental prayer. And now, by God's help, we must endeavor, like good gardeners, to make these plants grow. We should take care to water them, so they will not wither but bring forth flowers of such sweet fragrance as may please our Lord. Then He may take pleasure in often coming into this garden, and delighting Himself with our virtues.

92. Watering the Garden

These plants may be watered in four different ways: (1) By drawing water out of a well, and this cannot be done without much labor. (2) By using a wheel with buckets attached to it, and this can easily be turned by the hand. Sometimes I have in this way drawn water myself; I found that it was less troublesome and that it drew more than the former method. (3) By letting some small stream run into the garden; by this means it will be watered much better than by the preceding method. The earth will have more moisture, and there will be no necessity to water the ground so often. The labor of the gardener also will be much less. (4) By a good shower of rain falling, for then our Lord Himself waters the garden, without any labor on our part; and this is without comparison by far the best method. This comparison, which suits my purpose, may serve to explain in some measure the four degrees of prayer.

93. Step 1—Drawing Water From the Well

In this first part of our devotion we may in some degree help ourselves.

If the saints had never resolved to aspire to godliness and had not endeavored by degrees to execute their resolves, they would never have reached so high a state. His Majesty loves, and is a friend of, courageous souls, provided they proceed with humility, and have no confidence in themselves.... I am amazed when I consider how much is done in this way, by animating ourselves to do great things. Though the soul may not have sufficient strength to perform great things immediately, yet she takes a flight and mounts high, though, like a bird not yet well feathered, she grows tired and reposes herself.

Formerly I often considered what Saint Paul says: "I can do all things in him who strengthens me" (Phil 4:13). As for myself, I knew well I could do nothing.... Saint Peter lost nothing by throwing himself into the sea, though afterward he was afraid. These first resolutions are of great importance, though in this first degree it is necessary that we should proceed with discretion.

94. Step 2—Water Wheel: Quiet Prayer

The Master of the garden wishes that by means of the wheel and buckets the gardener might draw more water....

The soul begins to recollect itself and touch upon the supernatural, for it is impossible for her to acquire this gift by her own power. Yes, sometimes she may grow weary in turning round the wheel, working with the understanding, and filling the buckets. But as the water is higher in this second way, she has less labor than she had in drawing the water out of the well. I say the water is nearer to her, because grace is given to her, to know herself more clearly. This is done by collecting within herself all her faculties [the will, memory, and understanding]....

This water, the source of great blessings and favors that our Lord gives us, makes our virtues increase incomparably more than in the first degree of prayer, because the soul begins to rise out of her misery and have some small glimpse of the joys of eternal glory; this, I think, makes her increase the more in virtue, because she approaches nearer to that true power from which all virtues come—God.

95. Step 3—Flowing River: The Prayer of Union

I now speak of the third water wherewith this garden is watered, for this is a running water of a river or spring, and it waters with much less labor the garden, though the distribution of the water causes some trouble. But our Lord will so help the gardener, that in some degree the Lord will almost be the gardener Himself, and will do everything…. The pleasure, sweetness, and delight are greater beyond comparison than in the former state; the soul is so engulfed in the water of grace that she cannot go forward, nor does she know how, nor is she willing to return back, because of the excessive glory she enjoys.

O my God! In what state is a soul when she finds herself raised to this degree of prayer! She would wish to be changed into so many tongues, in order to praise You, O Lord! She utters a thousand holy extravagances, always endeavoring to please You, who hold her in this state.

96. Union and Service

The virtues obtained in this [third level of prayer] remain so much stronger in the soul than those obtained in the Prayer of Quiet that she cannot be ignorant of them. She sees herself quite another person, and she begins (though scarcely knowing how) to do great things by means of the odor the flowers yield of themselves; for now our Lord is pleased that the flowers should open....

The soul knows she possesses much quiet and peace, while on the other hand the memory and the understanding are so free that they are able to go about business and attend to works of charity. Now, though this may seem to be all the same as what I said regarding the Prayer of Quiet, yet it is different; there the soul is in such a state that she would fain not stir nor move, as she enjoys the holy leisure of Mary. But here, in the Prayer of Union, the soul may also imitate Martha. She performs, almost all together, the duties both of the active and the contemplative life, and she is able to attend to works of charity.

97. Step 4—The Occasional Rain Storm

In this fourth degree there is no suffering, but only enjoying, though yet without understanding what is enjoyed.... All the senses are occupied with this joy in such a manner that they cannot apply themselves to anything else, either interiorly or exteriorly....

When our Lord is beginning to bestow these favors, I thus address Him: "O Lord! Consider what You are doing: Do not forget so quickly my very grievous sins; and though You have forgotten them so far as to pardon them, yet remember them, I beseech You, so as to put some limit to Your favors. Do not place so precious a liquor in so broken a vessel, O my Creator! You have already seen how often I have spilt it. Commit not such a precious treasure to one in whom a desire for the consolations of this life has not yet been totally extinguished. How can You commit the strength of this city, and the keys of the fortress, to a cowardly commander, who, on the first attack of the enemy, is sure to let them enter? O my eternal King! Let not Your love of me be so great as to make You expose such precious jewels as these to danger."

98. If, in Confidence, You Should Fall…

Though a soul may arrive at such a degree as to induce our Lord to bestow many favors upon her in prayer, yet she must not place any confidence in herself, because she may fall….

But if she should fall, let her consider, and consider again, for the love of God, lest the devil should deceive her, by inducing her to omit mental prayer…. But let her trust in the goodness of God, which is greater than all the sins we can commit; and let her hope that He will not remember our ingratitude, when we wish to return to His friendship again…. Consider how He has proceeded with me, for I grew tired with offending His Majesty, before He grew tired with pardoning me. Never does He grow weary in giving. Never can His mercies be dried up. And so let us never grow weary of receiving His favors. May He be blessed forever, Amen. May all creatures praise Him.

99. Everyone Who Is Thirsty…

Fear not that our Lord will suffer you to die of thirst, for He it is who invites us to drink at His fountain. This I have already mentioned, and I repeat it often, because it tends greatly to frighten those who do not as yet know by experience the goodness of God, though by faith they know it. But it is a great blessing to have experienced the friendship and caresses He bestows on those who walk along this way, and how He defrays, as it were, all their expenses. And as for those who have not experienced this, I do not wonder at their desiring some security, that they will receive interest for what they give. Now you know there is a hundred-for-one return, even in this life, and that our Lord has said, "Ask, and you shall receive." If you do not believe His Majesty, who assures us of this in several parts of the gospel, then, sisters, it is no use my trying to persuade you of it. Yet if any doubt what I say, be assured that little is lost in trying it; for this way has this advantage, that more is given than is asked, or can be desired.

100. Enough Already

Some people have obtained the friendship of the Lord, for they make a good confession of their sins, and repent of them; but scarcely have two days passed by before they return to them again. Now, you may be sure, *this* is not the peace and friendship that the Spouse desires. Daughters, always endeavor not to be going every time to your confessor to acquaint him with the same fault. It is true we cannot be without faults, but at least let them be changed that they may not take root, for then it will be harder to eradicate them, and it may even be that from them many other roots spring. If we water every day a plant or shrub that we have set, it will grow so large that we shall afterward require a spade and ax to dig it up. And so it seems similar when we daily commit the same fault, however little it may be, if we do not correct it. But if it should be allowed to grow only one or ten days and then be rooted up immediately, all will be easy. This amendment you must beg of our Lord in prayer, for of ourselves we can do little.

Saint Jane Frances de Chantal
1572-1641

Jane, born to a wealthy French family, was happily married until she was widowed at age twenty-eight. She became a good friend of Bishop Francis de Sales and with him founded the Order of the Visitation of Mary, the first noncloistered order for women. Jane was a driving force behind de Sales' book *The Treatise on the Love of God.* Selections here are from her letters.

101. Give God a Free Hand

Your few words explaining your interior occupation have made your soul as clear to me as if it lay open before my eyes. All that passes within you and without you is God's own work.

Regarding your interior life, my advice is: Give God a free hand to do as He likes, while you look on in loving simplicity. And as to the exterior: Practice virtue by making faithful use from moment to moment of the opportunities provided by divine Providence. But it is superfluous for me to offer advice, as the heart that is governed by God needs no other guidance. Beseech of Him in His goodness, my dear daughter, to accomplish in us His holy will.

102. To a Mistress of Novices

Keep your heart on high and confide with holy joy, and no reserves, in the goodness of God. He has designed to make choice of you for His service in the monastery in which He has placed you: where no doubt there are others more capable than you, but that does not matter in God's eyes. It is humility, not capacity, He looks for. The most humble and the most faithful to His divine will contents Him most, and this is, I know, the way in which you are determined to serve Him. Live where you now are as you used to live at Nessy, growing in perfection by perseverance in the practice of virtue. This is all I ask of you. And if you give way now and again, be not cast down by such falls, but for love of God rise again with courage. It will give me great pleasure if you try to suppress childish ways. I wish I could make you see this. Should you, however, fall into them sometimes, do not worry.

103. Throw Yourself Upon the Mercy

Do you know that these fears and self-torturings about your past confessions are pure temptations of the devil? Make a firm stand and take no heed of them, dear daughter, for the devil is only trying in his malice to deceive you. Bear with his attacks and the suffering that comes of them gently and humbly, submitting to the good pleasure of God, who permits them to test your fidelity and confidence. Pay no regard to anything the tempter suggests. Never let your mind argue about it, but suffer it without yielding consent. Throw yourself upon the mercy of the divine Mercy. Leave to it the care of your salvation and of everything regarding you. Tell God that you have entire trust in His goodness, and although it may seem to you that you have not any [goodness], never cease to assure Him that you have, and always will have, with the assistance of His grace. Remain firm without wishing ever to confess past sins a second time, or ever swerving from your duty of patience and confidence in God, and you will see how God draws His glory and your good out of this temptation.

104. God's Present Presence

I have never been altogether without some slight and almost imperceptible feeling of the presence of God, by which in the midst of a storm of troubles and temptations my spirit never wholly loses its tranquillity; as long as I maintain myself in that presence my soul is calm notwithstanding the piteous struggle. When it first pleased our Lord to give me some relief in the terrible temptations under which I labored for so many years after I made my vow, I received the grace of a simple consciousness of His presence at prayer, and remaining in it I used to surrender myself up to Him and become absorbed and at rest in Him. This favor has not been withdrawn from me. Some days ago, our Lord gave me a light so vivid and set it before me in a manner so luminous that I saw without a shadow of doubt that I must no longer cast my eyes upon myself about anything whatsoever, nor even question my Beloved, but in all simplicity and repose become absorbed in Him. Now since this day of alleviation it seems to me that I have kept myself more continuously in God's presence, and I have but seldom had those violent temptations.

105. The Perfume of God

The evil spirit cannot give this attraction you speak of; he draws us away from good. On the other hand, our loving Savior sheds His perfume in our hearts, so that young souls may be drawn to follow Him by the sweetness of His odor.

Rejoice, then, in this grace with great humility.... Give yourself wholly into His hands. That done, have no fear of the evil spirit but of God alone, for, having quitted all things and yourself in your desire to belong to Him, Satan can do you no harm. Go forward quite simply, ruminating but little.... May God lead you Himself to the height of perfection to which He has called you, and always keep you within His holy hand. I never forget to ask this of His Goodness. Neither do you forget me when speaking to Him.

Blessed Marie of the Incarnation
1599-1672

The hardest thing widow Marie Martin ever did was to leave her eleven-year-old son with her sister in order to join the Ursuline convent at Tours, France. Her intense interior life has been compared with Saint Teresa's. Though she had originally intended to live a cloistered life, she followed a call to join the first women missionaries to Quebec, where she was a tireless servant leader.

106. The Creation and Creator

I discovered [God] in all creatures and in the ends for which He had created them, but in such a spiritual manner that this contemplation bore directly and uniquely on God so that the sight of the creatures did not distract me from Him. I had an infused knowledge of the nature of each thing and, not looking upon this as something extraordinary, I spoke about it at times in all simplicity. Addressing myself to the divine Majesty with the following passage in mind, *O God, thou hast made all things, and by thy will they have been created* (Rv 4:11), my soul conceived more than these [words] expressly state and its conception of them caused it to pour itself out in words of praise and of thanksgiving. And though my soul saw itself for what it was, an abject and vile creature in the presence of so great a majesty, still it was drawn toward the complete possession of that majesty.

107. The Agony and the Ecstasy

It seems to the soul that it has interior arms which are constantly extended to embrace [God]. And, as though it already possessed Him in this state of incessant striving for Him, it cries out, "My Beloved to me and I to Him. He is my good, He is another self to me, He is my all and my life." It is impossible to tell how love transforms the creature so as to cause it to run after the Beloved. It binds the creature with double chains; it holds it captive beneath its laws of love....

All the above can take place when one is on a journey, or during the distractions of one's occupations, and even during the course of necessary conversation with a number of persons, with as much application and attention of the mind as if one were in a chapel, for the soul is passively carried along by a divine touch, which begets in it a deeply rooted peace. But at the same time divine love keeps the soul in an agony which can indeed be felt but not described.

108. In the World but Not of It

[Before entering the convent] I realized that our Lord willed that I should be obliged to live in the world and He sweetened my sorrow through the remembrance of His words, *My yoke is easy and my burden light* (Mt 11:30). Then He rendered these words operative in my soul, with the result that my sorrow was soothed and I was made to run in His ways amidst the most earthly and material affairs. During such affairs my body was indeed taken up with them, but my spirit was bound to the most adorable Word Incarnate.... If it is necessary to speak to one's neighbor, one's regard does not turn away from [God], whom one loves. When the neighbor replies, the soul's colloquy with its Beloved is resumed, and attention to necessary matters does not distract it from [God]. The same is true in regard to writing, wherein the soul's attention has a double object—a divine one and the matter about which one is writing. The time spent dipping the pen into the ink is precious for the soul, for it devotes that time to colloquy (with its Beloved). Even if all the world were present, it could not divert the soul.

109. Union With Christ

In adoration of the Blessed Trinity, the Second Person of the Divine Word gave me to understand that He was truly the Spouse of the faithful soul. I understood this truth with certainty, and the insight into it that was granted me was a proximate preparation for seeing it actualized in myself. At that moment this most adorable Person took possession of my soul and, embracing it with an inexplicable love, united it to Himself and took it for His bride. When I say that He embraced it, this of course was not after the manner of human embraces. Nothing which falls within the scope of the senses is like this divine operation, but it is necessary for me to express myself in terms of our earthly life, since we are composed of matter. This transpired by means of divine touches and of a mutual compenetration in such wise that, no longer being myself, I abided in Him through intimacy of love and of union, so that I was lost to myself and no longer aware of myself, having become Him by participation. Then, for short moments, I was aware of myself and beheld the eternal Father and the Holy Spirit, and then the unity of the divine existence.

110. Always With a Greater Perfection

I've had various projects to manage since coming to Canada and hence I've had to deal with persons of diverse conditions, with the result that many thorny situations have arisen. On such occasions these divine maxims have always been my strength and my support. My manner of acting has often been regarded as due to my temperament, which some have spoken of as prompt to render help to others and to forget the annoyances which my neighbor might cause me. But these persons have not seen that my soul was possessed by the spirit of the maxims of the Son of God and that I acted in keeping with that spirit.

With the passing of time and the changes of spiritual states, the effects of the operations of the spirit of God change in a degree depending on the state upon which the soul enters. Thus a passage of Holy Scripture will at different times be operative in the soul of quite different effects, but always with a greater perfection, not indeed with regard to God, who is immutable, but in regard to the soul, which will increase in sanctity until the end of life.

Blessed Mary
of Agreda
1602-1665

Mary, a long-term abbess of a Discalced Franciscan convent in Spain, wrote, burned, and then rewrote a very popular tome titled *Mystical City of God*, an extended "life of Mary" based on visions and voices and, she admits, possibly a bit of imagined embellishment.

111. The Finger of God

O Holy Spirit, adorable and all-powerful, the Holy Church calls you the Finger of God, because you proceed from the Father and the Son, as the finger from the body and the arm. You are God, like the Father and the Son, infinite, eternal, and immense. Ah! Triumph over the wickedness of men, and by the merits of Jesus Christ and His divine Mother, communicate to us your gifts. Amen.

112. Mary's Humility

[Mary] was known and recognized as the Mother of that Master, so famous throughout Palestine for the wonders He had wrought. This was a great glory for Mary, yet under it, she humbled herself more profoundly than all the saints have ever done, and she endeavored to prevent the honors which were sometimes rendered to her when she was present at the miracles of our Lord. The evangelists have written of two occasions. A woman cried out in honor of the Blessed Virgin: Blessed is the womb that bore You! Hearing these words, Mary interiorly prayed her divine Son to turn this praise from her, which He did by the words: "Blessed are they who hear the word of God, and keep it" [Mk 3:35]. The other occasion was that recorded in Luke 8. Seeing the glory that would be rendered to her by the great concourse of people crowded to hear her divine Son, she again prayed interiorly that He would save her from it.

The Lord heard her prayer. When a voice cried out, "Behold Your Mother and Your brethren," He answered, "My Mother and My brethren are they who hear My word and keep it."

113. The Way to the Cross

The sun had already risen when the Blessed Mother resolved to leave her retreat, to follow the steps of her Son.

They quitted the house, and as they passed through the streets, Mary heard the conversations going on among the people about her divine Son, yet, far from being indignant at those who spoke ill of Him, she prayed for them.

From her garments, many people recognized her to be the Mother of Jesus. Some were moved with feelings of natural compassion for her, others insulted her, saying that she had given her Son a bad education. Hearing a great noise and tumult, Mary looked, and beheld her innocent Son in the hands of the rabble; prostrating herself upon the ground, she adored Him; at the same moment there passed between them looks that penetrated their hearts with inexpressible grief, and they spoke with each other from the interior of their souls. Then, as they dragged Jesus to Pilate, the afflicted Mother, bathed in tears, followed with the pious women, exclaiming, "My Son, my beloved Son!"

114. Mary at Pentecost

It is impossible to imagine the loving solicitude of the Blessed Virgin, or her ardent charity in strengthening the weakness of that pious yet still imperfect assembly [in the Upper Room]. The apostles themselves doubted the coming of the Holy Spirit; as the Mother of piety, she came to their aid, and dissipated their doubts, when, feeble and vacillating, they said that the Holy Ghost would not come as had been promised. With great charity she reassured them, saying, "All that my divine Son said has been entirely accomplished; He said in particular, that He would suffer and rise again, and all has been verified. If, then, He has promised to send the consoling Spirit, without doubt He will come to console and sanctify us." At these words they became so united, that from that time there was not the slightest discord in this devoted assembly; they were all of one heart and one soul, and had but one sentiment and one will.

115. Temptation of Aging Mary

Having transformed themselves into angels of light, the whole army of dragons entered into Mary's oratory. Lucifer was the first to speak, and his words were full of his venom, which is pride. "You are all-powerful, O Mary! Great and courageous among women. The whole world honors and glorifies you, because of the marvelous virtues it knows you to possess, and the great wonders you operate. You are worthy of this glory, as no other person is equal to you in sanctity."

While he, with his false tongue, uttered these incontestable truths, he endeavored to raise in her imagination thoughts of complacency. But all his arrows fell harmless on her humble heart, for all the torments of the martyrs would have caused her less sensible pain than these evil suggestions. To repulse them she made frequent acts of profound humility. Beholding this heroic annihilation of herself, Lucifer cried out to his companions, "Ah! The pains of hell are less torment to me than the profound humility of this great woman!" Then crushed and vanquished by her, they threw themselves into the abyss, and the august Mother returned thanks to the Most High for this first victory.

Jeanne Marie D.L.M. Guyon
1648-1717

To survive a difficult marriage, Jeanne turned inward, seeking intimate union with God. Widowed young, well spoken and educated, she gained an impressive audience for—and severe opposition to—her personal spirituality, eventually spending years in the French Bastille prison. Her many writings include *The Short Method of Prayer*.

116. Faith and Glory

A man is far from experiencing the full grace of God who desires martyrdom but is restless under the yoke of divine Providence, which places martyrdom beyond his reach and requires him to glorify God in the humblest and most retired avocations of life. The true desire, the right desire, is that which comes in the divine order, and the divine order can never be known and appreciated except in connection with a knowledge of the developments of the present moment. At one time the apostle Paul made tents in God's order; at another time, in the same divine order, he preached eloquently on Mars' Hill at Athens. In both cases he glorified God equally. If we are right in motive and right in place, exercising all the requisite faith in God at the same time, *all will be well.*

117. Perilous Travels—God's Mercy

How wonderful, O my God, at this as at many other times, has been Your protection over me! How many perils have I passed through in going over mountains, and on the edges of steep and terrible cliffs! How often have You checked the foot of the mule, already slipping over the precipice. How often have I been exposed to be thrown headlong from frightful heights into hideous torrents, which, though rolling in ravines far below our shrinking sight, forced us to hear them by their horrible noise. You, O God, did guard me in such imminent dangers. When the dangers were most manifest, then was my faith in You strongest. In You my soul trusted. I felt that if it were Your will that I should be dashed headlong down the rocks, or drowned in the waters, or brought to the end of my life in any other way, it would all be well; the will of God, whatever it might be in relation to me, making everything equal.

118. Sorrow as Evidence of Faith

In regard to the principle of faith, I will further say that it sometimes lies latent, as it were, and concealed in the midst of discomfort and sorrow. I recollect that in the former periods of my experience I once spent a considerable time in a state of depression and deep sorrow, because I supposed I had lost God, or at least had lost His favor. My grief was great and without cessation. If I had seen things as I now see them, and had understood them then as I now understand them, I should have found a principle of restoration and of comfort in the very grief that overwhelmed me. How could I thus have mourned the loss of God's presence, or rather what seemed to me to be such loss, if I did not love Him? And how could I love Him without faith in Him? In my sorrow, therefore, I might have found the evidence of my faith. And it is a great truth, that in reality, whatever may at times be the appearance, God never does desert, and never can desert, those who believe.

119. Water Compared to the Soul

Nothing is more simple than water; nothing is more pure. In this respect it may be regarded as an emblem of the holy soul. But this is not all. Among other things, water is the property of yielding readily and easily to all impressions that can be made upon it. And here we have another striking incident of resemblance. As water yields with inconceivable readiness to the slightest human touch, so does the holy soul yield, without any resistance, to the slightest touch of God; that is, to the slightest intimations of the divine will. Again, water is without color, but it is susceptible of all colors. So the holy soul, colorless in itself, reflects the hues, whatever they may be, that emanate from the divine countenance. Again, water has no form, but takes the form of the vessels, almost endless in variety, in which it is contained. So the holy soul takes no position or form of itself, but only that which God gives it.

120. Prison Prayer

I, being in the Bastille, prayed: O my God, if You are pleased to render me a spectacle to men and angels, Your holy will be done! All that I ask is that You will be with and save those who love You, so that neither life nor death, neither principalities nor powers, may ever separate them from the love of God which is in Jesus Christ. As for me, what matters it what men think of me, or what they make me suffer, because they cannot separate me from that Savior whose name is engraved in the very bottom of my heart? If I can only be accepted of Him, I am willing that all men should despise and hate me. Their strokes will polish what may be defective in me, so that I may be presented in peace to Him, for whom I die daily. Without His favor, I am wretched. O Savior! I present myself before You an offering, a sacrifice. Purify me in Your blood, that I may be accepted by You.

ACKNOWLEDGMENTS

SAINT HILDEGARD OF BINGEN

Selections 3, 4, 5, 6, 7, 8: from HILDEGARD OF BINGEN, by Mother Columba Hart and Jane Bishop © 1990 by the Abbey of Regina Laudis: Benedictine Congregation Regina Laudis of the Strict Observance Inc. Used by permission of Paulist Press.

MECHTILD OF MAGDEBURG

All selections: from MECHTILD OF MAGDEBURG, translated and introduced by Frank Tobin © 1998 by Frank Tobin. Used by permission of Paulist Press.

HADEWIJCH

All selections: from HADEWIJCH, translated and introduced by Mother Columba Hart, O.S.B. © 1980 by The Missionary Society of St. Paul the Apostle in the State of New York. Used by permission of Paulist Press.

BLESSED MARGARET EBNER

All selections: from MARGARET EBNER, translated and edited by Leonard P. Hindsley © 1993 by Leonard P. Hindsley. Used by permission of Paulist Press.

SAINT CATHERINE OF SIENA

Selections 74, 77, 78: from CATHERINE OF SIENA, translation and introduction by Suzanne Noffke, O.P. © 1990 by The Missionary Society of St. Paul the Apostle in the State of New York. Used by permission of Paulist Press.

Life and Doctrine of Saint Catherine of Genoa. New York: Catholic Publication Society, 1874.

Life of Saint Teresa, by Saint Teresa, translated by John Dalton. New York: P.J. Kenedy, 1851.

The Way of Perfection and *Conceptions of Divine Love,* by Saint Teresa, translated by John Dalton. London: C. Dolman, 1852.

Selected Letters of Saint Jane Frances de Chantal, translated by the Sisters of the Visitation. London: R. & T. Washbourne, 1918.

Divine Life of the Most Holy Virgin Mary (an abridgement of *Mystical City of God*), by Mary of Agreda, translated by Joseph Boullan. Philadelphia: Peter Cunningham, 1872.

Life of Madame de la Mothe Guyon, by Thomas Upham. New York: Fleming H. Revell, 1905.

Sincere thanks to Father Joseph Tylenda, S.J., of the Woodstock Theological Library, Georgetown University, for his smile and research help.